This book belongs to

Name: _____

www.a4ace.com   www.math-knots.com

Cover Design by :
Gowri Vemuri

First Edition :
May, 2019

Author :
Gowri Vemuri

Edited by :
Ritvik Pothapragada

Questions: mathknots.help@gmail.com

NOTE : VDOE is neither affiliated nor sponsors or endorses this product.

This book is dedicated to:

My Mom, who is my best critic, guide and supporter.

To what I am today, and what I am going to become tomorrow,

is all because of your blessings, unconditional affection and support.

This book is dedicated to the

strongest women of my life ,

my dearest mom

and

to all those moms in this universe.

G.V.

The Virginia Board of Education and Virginia Department of Education (VDOE) have developed the Virginia Assessment Program (VAP) to measure and evaluate students' academic progress in the Standards of Learning (SOLs). The SOLs indicate Virginia's expectations for what students should know and be able to do in the subject areas of reading, writing, mathematics, science, and history/social science.

Students in grades 3-12 to take the Standards of Learning (SOL) assessments each year. Some of the tests are required by all students each year, and others are required only at specific grade levels. Additionally, with the removal of some SOL tests in recent years, the VDOE assigned the responsibility of the creation and administration of alternate, performance - based assessments on local divisions. Student scores from these tests determine a school's and the division's state accreditation and measures progress toward meeting federal targets.

Virginia Standards of Learning (SOL) tests are generally given online unless a student has an identified and documented need to be assessed using paper,pencil format. The test question format is typically multiple choice, and each test contains some technology enhanced items.

GRADE 3-8 STANDARDS OF LEARNING(SOL) TESTS

GRADE 3	GRADE 4	GRADE 5	GRADE 6	GRADE 7	GRADE 8
	VIRGINIA STUDIES				WRITING
MATH	MATH	MATH	MATH	MATH	MATH
READING	READING	READING	READING	READING	READING
		SCIENCE			SCIENCE

NOTE : VDOE is neither affiliated nor sponsors or endorses this product.

7   www.a4ace.com   www.math-knots.com

END OF COURSE STANDARDS OF LEARNING (SOL) TESTS

GRADE 9	GRADE 10	GRADE 11
ALGEBRA I	GEOMETRY	ALGEBRA II
EARTH SCIENCE	BIOLOGY	CHEMISTRY
WORLD HISTORY I	WORLD HISTORY II	VIRGINIA & US HSTORY
		WORLD GEOGRAPHY
		ENGLISH : READING
		ENGLISH : WRITING

Any Student taking one of the courses listed here is expected to take the corresponding end-of-course SOL test. The grade levels depicted here represent grade level at which students typically participate in these courses.

NOTE : VDOE is neither affiliated nor sponsors or endorses this product.

SOL Test Scoring and Performance Reports:

Standards of Learning assessments in English reading, mathematics, science and history/social science are made up of 35-50 items or questions that measure content knowledge, scientific and mathematical processes, reasoning and critical thinking skills. English writing skills are measured with a two-part assessment that includes multiple-choice items and an essay.

Student performance is graded on a scale of 0-600 with 400 representing the minimum level of acceptable proficiency and 500 representing advanced proficiency. On English reading and mathematics tests, the Board of Education has defined three levels of student achievement: basic, proficient, and advanced, with basic describing progress towards proficiency.

Performance Achievement Levels:

- The achievement levels for grades 3-8 reading and mathematics tests are: *Pass/Advanced, Pass/Proficient, Fail/Basic,* and *Fail/Below Basic.*

- The achievement levels for science tests, history tests, and End-of-Course (EOC) tests* are: *Pass/Advanced, Pass/Proficient,* and *Fail/Does Not Meet.*

- The EOC Writing (2010 SOL) test, EOC Reading (2010 SOL) test, and EOC Algebra II (2009 SOL) test have an achievement level of *Advanced/College Path* in place of the *Pass/Advanced* achievement level.

NOTE : VDOE is neither affiliated nor sponsors or endorses this product.

INDEX

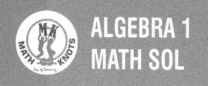
FORMULA SHEET

1. Area of a triangle

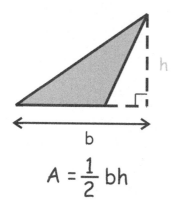

$$A = \frac{1}{2} bh$$

2. Area of a parellelogram

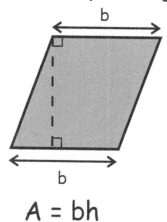

$$A = bh$$

3. Volume and Surface area of a Cuboid

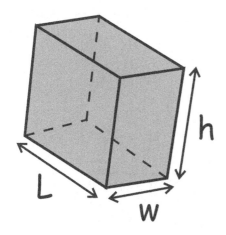

$$V = lwh$$
$$S.A = 2(lw + lh + wh)$$

4. volume and Surface area of a Cone

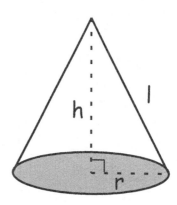

$$V = \frac{1}{3} \Pi r^2$$
$$S.A = \Pi r(l + h)$$

5. Perimeter and Area of a Square

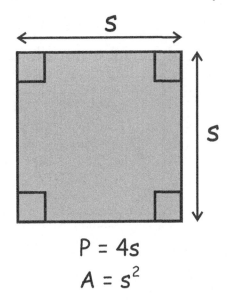

$$P = 4s$$
$$A = s^2$$

6. Area of a Trapezium

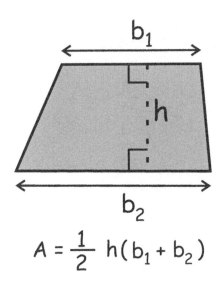

$$A = \frac{1}{2} h(b_1 + b_2)$$

7. Volume and Surface area of a Cylinder

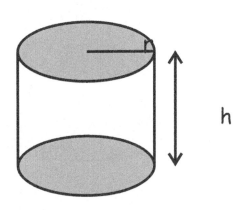

$$V = \Pi r^2 h$$
$$S.A = 2\Pi r(h+r)$$

8. Volume and Surface area of a Pyramid

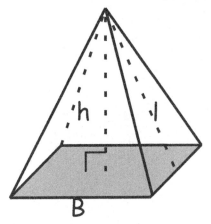

$$V = \frac{1}{3} Bh$$
$$S.A = \frac{1}{2} lp + B$$

9. Circumference and Area of a Circle

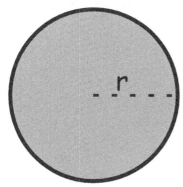

$c = 2\pi r$

$A = \pi r^2$

pi

$\pi = 3.14$

$\pi = \dfrac{22}{7}$

10. Right angled Triangle (Pythagoran)

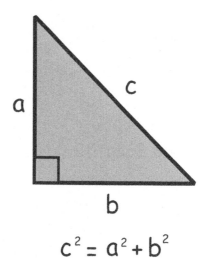

$c^2 = a^2 + b^2$

Pythagorean triplets
Examples : (3 , 4 , 5)
(5 , 12 , 13)
(7 , 24 , 25)
(15 , 20 , 25)
(6 , 8 , 10)
(9 , 12 , 15)
(6 , 8 , 10)
(12 , 16 , 20)
(10 , 24 , 26)

11. Perimeter and Area of a Rectangle

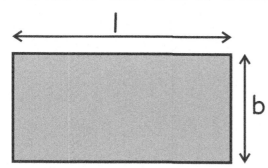

Area = l b $\times$

Perimeter = 2(l + b)

15   www.a4ace.com   www.math-knots.com

12. Quadratic formula

$$x = \frac{-b \pm \sqrt{b^2 - 4ac}}{2a}$$

13. Algebraic Identities

$$(a + b)^2 = a^2 + 2ab + b^2$$

$$(a - b)^2 = a^2 - 2ab + b^2$$

$$a^2 - b^2 = (a + b)(a - b)$$

$$a^2 + b^2 = (a + b)^2 - 2ab$$

$$a^2 + b^2 = (a - b)^2 + 2ab$$

14. Equation of a Straight line

$$y = mx + c$$
Where m = slope
c = y - intercept

www.a4ace.com   www.math-knots.com

Abbreviations

milligram	mg		volume	V
gram	g		total Square Area	S.A
kilogram	kg		area of base	B
milliliter	mL		ounce	oz
liter	L		pound	lb
kiloliter	kL		quart	qt
millimeter	mm		gallon	gal.
centimeter	cm		inches	in.
meter	m		foot	ft
kilometer	km		yard	yd
square centimeter	cm^2		mile	mi.
cubic centimeter	cm^3		square inch	sq in.

square foot	sq ft
cubic inch	cu in.
cubic foot	cu ft

year	yr
month	mon
hour	hr
minute	min
second	sec

         www.a4ace.com   www.math-knots.com

ALGEBRA 1
SOL
Practice Test - 4

www.a4ace.com   www.math-knots.com

1. Solve for v

    $$3 (1 + 2v) = -3 (5 - 5v)$$

    (A) 0   (B) 5   (C) -1   (D) 2

2. If $f(k) = \dfrac{k}{2} - 4$ then which of the below best describes the graph f(k)

    (A) Slope = 1 , y-intercept = -4   (B) Slope = $\dfrac{1}{2}$, y-intercept = -4

    (C) Slope = $\dfrac{-1}{2}$, y-intercept = 4   (D) Slope = 1 , y-intercept = 4

3. Find the slope of the line in the graph below

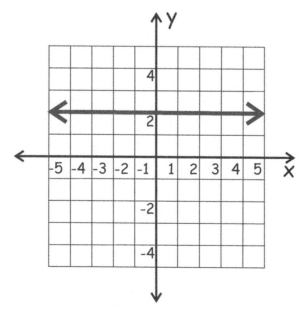

    (A)   -5   (B)   5

    (C)   -3   (D)   0

 www.a4ace.com   www.math-knots.com

4. Which of the below order pair is the solution of the below system of equations ?

$$p - 2q = -6$$
$$4p - q = 4$$

(A) (2, -4)   B) (-4, -1)   (C) (2, 4)   (D) (-2, 4)

5. $2(m + 3) - m > - 21 - 8m$

(A) m <= 3   (B) m > -3   (C) m >= 6   (D) m > 3

6. The equation of the line 'm' is represented by which of the below options ?

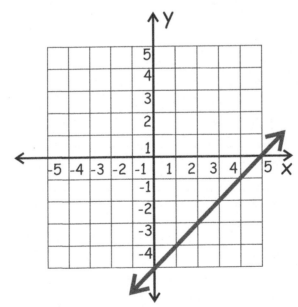

(A) y = x - 5   (B) y = -4x - 5

(C) y = -5x + 1   (D) y = 4x - 5

22

7. Which of the below quadratic equation has roots of -3 and 5 ?

    (A) $p^2 - 2p - 15 = 0$ (B) $p^2 + 2p + 15 = 0$

    (C) $p^2 + 2p - 15 = 0$ (D) $p^2 + 8p + 15 = 0$

8. Which graph best represents the equation

    $$y = -5x + 3$$

(A)
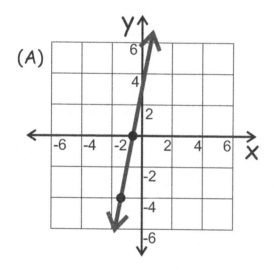

(B)
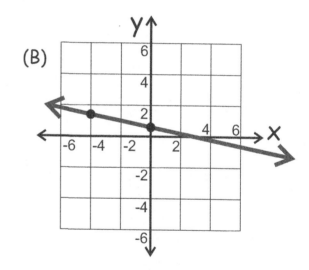

(C)
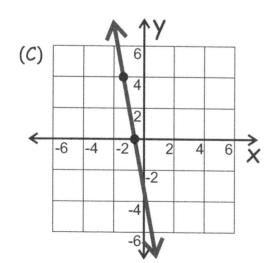

(D)
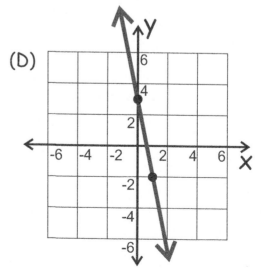

9. System of linear equations are shown in the graph below. Which of the below is the solution of the system of linear equations ?

$$y = \frac{-1}{2} x + 3$$

$$y = \frac{-5}{2} x + 7$$

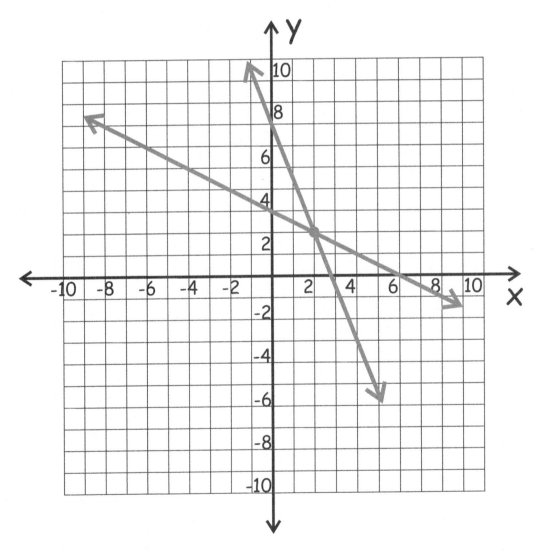

(A) (2 , -2)

(B) (2 , 2)

(C) (-2 , 2)

(D) (-2 , 8)

 www.a4ace.com   www.math-knots.com

10. Which of the below represents distributive property ?

   (A) $9(-4 + 6n) = 54n + 36$ (B) $54n - 36 = 54n + 36$

   (C) $-9(-4 + 6n) = -54n + 36$ (D) $9(-4 + 6n) = 3(-12 - 18n)$

11. Which of the below graphs represents the equation of the straight line represented as

$$y = x - 5$$

(A)
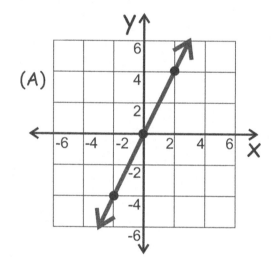

(B)
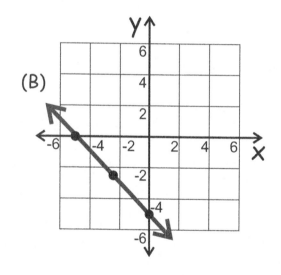

(C)
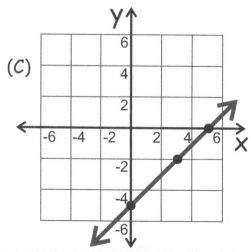

(D)
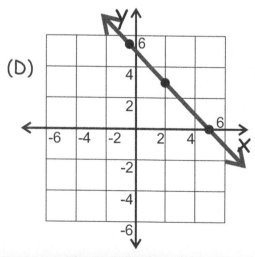

12.   Sammy buys a car for $21,000 from his savings and spends 25$ on gas every week from his savings account. If there are no deposits into his savings account ,after w weeks the amount(T) spent is obtained by the below equation.

$$T = 25w + 21,000$$

What is the slope of the equation ?

(A) 21,000   (B) -5,250

(C) 25   (D) -25

13.   Roots of the below equation are

$$x^2 - 15x + 56 = 0$$

(A)   (7 , 6)
(B)   (8 , 7)
(C)   (-5 , 4)
(D)   (4 , -5)

14.   Find the equation of the straight line with slope = -6 and containing the point (-2 , -10)

(A) $y = \frac{x}{6} - 22$ (B) $y = \frac{x}{3} + 22$

(C) $y = -6x + 22$ (D) $y = -6x - 22$

15. Which of the below inequalities is same as 3m - 2n > 6

    (A) $n < -3 + \frac{3}{2} m$ (B) $n > \frac{3}{2} - m$

    (C) $n < 8m - 1$ (D) $n < \frac{m}{2} - \frac{3}{4}$

16. What is the slope of the line that passes through

    (-19 , -14) , (-3 , 14)

    (A) $\frac{-7}{4}$ (B) $\frac{-4}{7}$

    (C) $\frac{7}{4}$ (D) $\frac{4}{7}$

17. Heather sold half of her bracelets and then made fourteen more. She now has 49. How many bracelets were on sale originally?

    (A) 60
    (B) 70
    (C) 28
    (D) 35

18.   Zara and Julia are selling brownies and cupcakes for a school fund raiser. 2 brownies and a cupcakes for a total of $6. A brownie and three cupcakes cost a total of $8. What is the cost of one brownie ?

(A) $2
(B) $5
(C) $1.50
(D) $0.75

19.   Evaluate $Z^2 - (\dfrac{Y}{2} - Z)$; Where Y = 10 and Z = 6

(A)   28
(B)   39
(C)   44
(D)   37

20.   Evaluate the below

$$(50 \times 10^6) (0.052 \times 10^0)$$

(A) 9.615×10^{-6}

(B) 26×10^{26}

(C) 2.6×10^6

(D) 9.615×10^8

         www.a4ace.com   www.math-knots.com

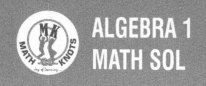
21. Simplify the expression
$$(10n^5 + 4n^4 - 11n^2) + (-11n^5 - 5n^4 - 5n^2)$$

(A) $-15n^5 + 17n^4 - 16n^2$

(B) $-15n^5 + 4n^4 - 16n^2$

(C) $-15n^5 - n^4 - 16n^2$

(D) $-n^5 - n^4 - 16n^2$

22. Simplest radical form of $\sqrt{245}$ is ?

(A) $7\sqrt{5}$

(B) 7

(C) $7\sqrt{7}$

(D) $5\sqrt{7}$

23. Evaluate the polynomial to simplest form where $x \neq 0$
$$(8p^5 + 8p^4 + 2p^3) \div 4p^3$$

(A) $3 + \dfrac{1}{4p} + \dfrac{4}{p^2}$

(B) $3 + \dfrac{4}{p} + \dfrac{1}{4p^2}$

(C) $\dfrac{p^2}{4} + 4p + \dfrac{1}{4}$

(D) $2p^2 + 2p + \dfrac{1}{2}$

24. Factorize the below quadratic expression completely ?
$$3b^2 + 28b + 49$$

(A) $(7b - 1)(b + 2)$

(B) $(7b - 10)(b - 3)$

(C) $(3b + 7)(b + 7)$

(D) $(b + 7)(3b - 7)$

25. A number decreased by 15 is greater than 17

    (A) $n^2 > 17$

    (B) $15 - n > 17$

    (B) $15 + n > 17$

    (D) $n - 15 > 17$

26. Evaluate the polynomial
    $$2p(3p^2 + 8p + 5)$$

    (A) $56p^4 + 14p^3 + 42p^2$

    (B) $4p^2 - 2p + 6$

    (C) $6p^3 + 16p^2 + 10p$

    (D) $28p^4 - 16p^3 + 24p^2$

27. Which labeled point on the number line is closed to $\sqrt{620}$

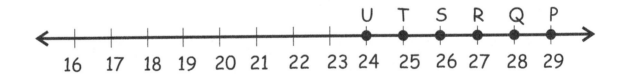

    (A) U   (B) S   (C) Q   (D) T

28. Length of a hockey stick is 87221.37×10^{-3} inches. While playing Tony breaks it to a length 87.154×10^0 inches. What is the length of the other broken piece ?

    (A) 6.737×10^{-2}

    (B) 67.34×10^{-2}

    (C) 66.034×10^{-3}

    (D) 67.34×10^{-3}

 www.a4ace.com   www.math-knots.com

29. Factorize the below quadratic expression completely ?
$$-7k^2 - 5k$$

   (A) $-3k(7k + 15)$ (B) $-k(7k + 15)$

   (C) $-k(7k + 1)$ (D) $-k(7k + 5)$

30. A number decreased by 5 is equal to 42

   (A) $5n = 42$ (B) $n - 5 = 42$

   (C) $5 - n = 42$ (D) $5^2 >= 42$

31. The function $f(x) = \$23.43 + x$; After paying $2.02 for a sandwich, Henry has $23.43. How much money does he had originally ?

   (A) $ 25.45

   (B) $ 21.41

   (C) $ 20.42

   (D) $ 25.47

                   www.a4ace.com   www.math-knots.com

32. Which of the below equation represents the relationship between time and number of hoops made ?

Time in minutes (t)	Hoops (h)
5	8
10	16
15	24
20	32
25	40

(A) $h = \dfrac{8}{5}t$

(B) $h = 8 + t$

(C) $h = \dfrac{5t}{8}$

(D) $5t - 8$

33. Find the domain of the relation shown from the below data set ?

X	y
3	33
1	21
11	71
2	26
5	38

(A) { -33 , 21 , 71 , 26 , 38 }

(B) { -23 , 21 , 11 , 2 , 5 }

(C) { 3 , 1 , 11 , 2 , 5 }

(D) { -3 , -1 , 71 , 2 , 5 }

34. 2,154 juice boxes can be packed in 6 cartons of same size. how many juice boxes can be packed in 13 such cartons ?

    (A) 3666   (B) 4667

    (C) 4664   (D) 5660

35. Which of the below order pairs data set represents a function ?

    (A) { (2 , 93) , (4 , 83) , (5 , 76) , (2 , 54) , (11 , 34) }

    (B) { (5 , 93) , (4 , 83) , (5 , 76) , (8 , 54) , (11 , 34) }

    (C) { (2 , 93) , (4 , 83) , (5 , 76) , (8 , 54) , (4 , 34) }

    (D) { (2 , 93) , (4 , 83) , (5 , 76) , (8 , 54) , (11 , 34) }

36. Evaluate f(3) , where $f(x) = 7x^2 - 3x + 11$

    (A) 55

    (B) 25

    (C) 65

    (D) 85

37. What is the domain of the function y = x - 1 represented by the below graph ?

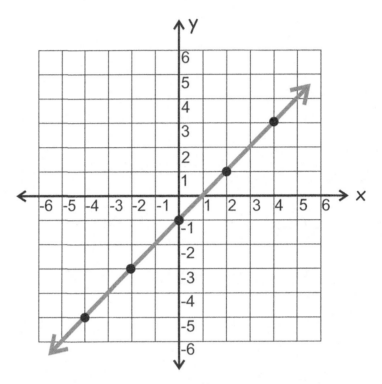

(A)   D = {-4 , -2 , 0 , 2 , 4 }

(B)   D = {2.8 , 0.4 , 1.1 , 5.5 , 5.2 }

(C)   D = {0.8 , 1.3 , -0.5 , 3.5 , -9.9 }

(D)   D = {-5, 0.5 , 6.5 , 6 , -10 }

38. What is the range of the function $f(x) = 3x^4 + 1$
where Domain = { -4 , -2 , 0 , 3 }

(A) { 194 , -49 , 1 , 204}   (B) { 193 , 49 , -1 , -244}

(C) { 769 , 49 , 1 , 244}   (D) { 194 , 48 , 11 , 204}

34

39. Which graph best represents a direct variation ?

$$y = \frac{1}{2}x$$

(A)

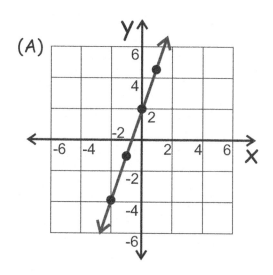

(B)

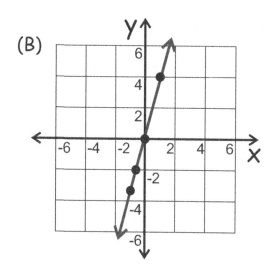

(C)

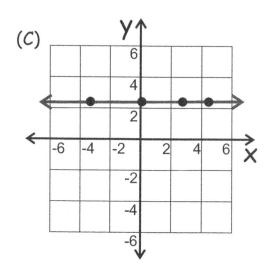

(D)

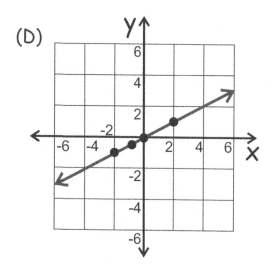

40. Which of the below tables shows the relation between X and Y as direct variation.

(A)

X	Y
1	14
5	24
10	46
15	71
20	80

(B)

X	Y
1	41
5	27
10	70
15	30
20	67

(C)

X	Y
1	4
5	20
10	40
15	60
20	80

(D)

X	Y
1	1
5	4
10	11
15	14
20	22

41. Cost of each art piece in the art exhibition is shown in the below table.

# of Art pieces (P)	sale prices $(S)
1	12.50
4	50
8	100
10	125
12	150

Which of the below gives the total price (t) of p art pieces ?

(A) t = 12.5 p

(B) t = 12.5 - p

(C) t = 15 + p

(D) t = 10 p

42. Which of the below graph best represents the function
$$f(x) = x^2 - 7x + 10$$

(A)
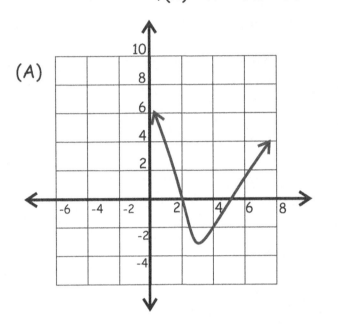

(B)
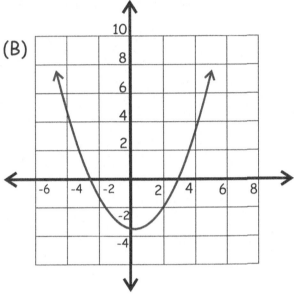

(C)
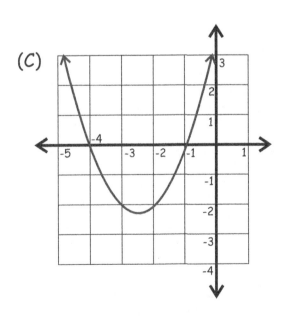

(D)
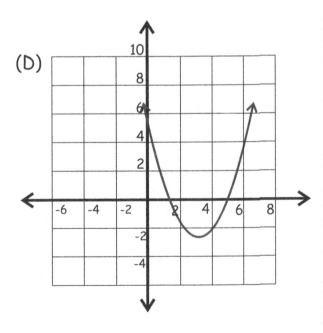

43. Find the sum of the matrices ?

$$\begin{vmatrix} 7 & 6 \\ -4 & -2 \\ 8 & 3 \end{vmatrix} \; + \; \begin{vmatrix} 8 & 1 \\ -3 & 5 \\ 7 & -7 \end{vmatrix}$$

(A) $\begin{vmatrix} -1 & 8 \\ 5 & 4 \\ 19 & -5 \end{vmatrix}$

(B) $\begin{vmatrix} 5 & -10 \\ -11 & 16 \\ 20 & -5 \end{vmatrix}$

(C) $\begin{vmatrix} 25 & 17 \\ -2 & 8 \\ 10 & 16 \end{vmatrix}$

(D) $\begin{vmatrix} 15 & 7 \\ -7 & 3 \\ 15 & -4 \end{vmatrix}$

44. The table below shows the snow fall in various cities in USA during June.

June rain fall in inches

Day	Virginia	Delaware	Richmond	Maryland
Monday	21	5	7	0
Tuesday	11	19	13	2
Wednesday	9	12	5	9
Thursday	13	4	8	1
Friday	1	3	20	10
Saturday	4	4	1	16
Sunday	6	18	14	13

Which state had the greatest average rain fall during this week ?

(A) Delaware

(B) Virginia

(C) Richmond

(D) Maryland

45. Which equation is the line of best fit for the data in the below table ?

X	Y
10	-7
5	-4
0	-1
-5	2
-10	5

(A) $Y = \dfrac{-3x}{5} - 1$

(B) $Y = \dfrac{-3x}{5} + 1$

(C) $Y = \dfrac{3x}{5} + 2$

(D) $Y = \dfrac{3x}{5}$

 www.a4ace.com

www.math-knots.com

46. Which graph best represents the below data ?

Average price per pound

Vegetables	Price
Collards	62
Iceburg lettuce	85
Rutabaga	90
Corn	80
Okra	55
Bell pepper	75
Spinach	44
Sweet potato	90
Carrots	70
Cherry tomato	65
Sweet Banana pepper	72
Swiss Chard	70

Vegetables	Price
Grape Tomato	65
Kentucky Wonder Bean	65
Jersey Tomato	74
Peanut	120
Shallots	115
Cabbage	50
Gooseneck Gourd	120
Zucchini	50
Walla walla onion	85
Red lettuce	50

(A)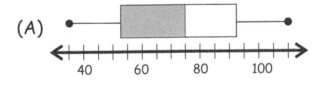

(B)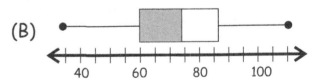

(C)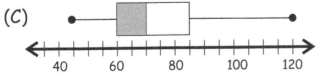

(D)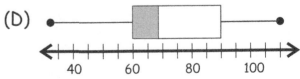

47. Which graph best represents a direct variation

$$y = \frac{1}{4} x + 2$$

(A)
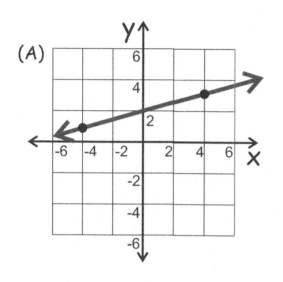

(B)
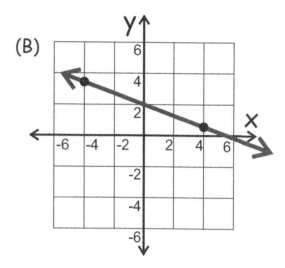

(C)
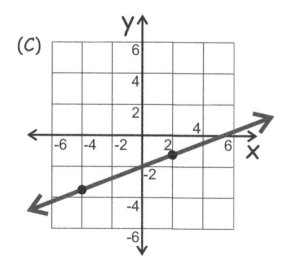

(D)
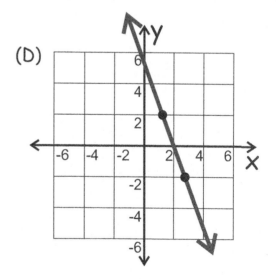

48. Rik solved below number of math problems each week

20 , 94 , 36 , 98 , 41 , 97 , 89 , 29

He then solved 45 more after the week . How are the mean and median affected ?

(A) The mean increased and the median increased.
(B) The median decreased and the mean is decreased.
(C) The median and the mean both remained the same.
(D) The mean increased and the median decreased

49. Rock and Roll theme park charges a flat rate of $18 plus a price based on the purchaser age. The table below shows various ages and their associated prices.

Age	No. of tickets	Age	No. of tickets
7 - 10	25	19 - 22	55
11 - 14	11	23 - 26	47
15 - 18	38	27 - 30	35

Which of the below represents the total money collected ?

(A) $18 \begin{vmatrix} 25 & 55 \\ 11 & 47 \\ 38 & 35 \end{vmatrix}$

(B) $7 \begin{vmatrix} 55 & 32 \\ 48 & 41 \\ 63 & 59 \end{vmatrix}$

(C) $10 \begin{vmatrix} 25 & 30 \\ 45 & 39 \\ 42 & 68 \end{vmatrix}$

(D) $20 \begin{vmatrix} 38 & 41 \\ 56 & 21 \\ 56 & 77 \end{vmatrix}$

ALGEBRA 1
MATH SOL

TEST - 4

50. Evaluate the below matrices

$$\begin{vmatrix} 1 & 2 \\ 3 & 4 \\ 5 & 6 \end{vmatrix} + \begin{vmatrix} 7 & 8 \\ 9 & 10 \\ 11 & 12 \end{vmatrix} = ?$$

(A) $\begin{vmatrix} 14 & 7 \\ 0 & -13 \\ 15 & -21 \end{vmatrix}$

(B) $\begin{vmatrix} -15 & -2 \\ 6 & 3 \\ -3 & 4 \end{vmatrix}$

(C) $\begin{vmatrix} 8 & 10 \\ 12 & 14 \\ 16 & 18 \end{vmatrix}$

(D) $\begin{vmatrix} -9 & 15 \\ 7 & 17 \\ 15 & -1 \end{vmatrix}$

     www.a4ace.com   www.math-knots.com

ALGEBRA 1
SOL
Practice Test - 5

www.a4ace.com   www.math-knots.com

1.   Solve for p from the below equation

$$5 (4p + 7) = (6p - 11) 3$$

(A) 34   (B) 39   (C) -36   (D) -34

2.   If $f(k) = -\dfrac{2k}{5} - \dfrac{7}{5}$ then which of the below best describes the graph f(k)

(A) Slope = $\dfrac{2}{5}$, y-intercept = $\dfrac{-7}{5}$ (B) Slope = -2 , y-intercept = $\dfrac{-7}{5}$

(C) Slope = $\dfrac{-2}{5}$, y-intercept = $\dfrac{-7}{5}$ (D) Slope = $\dfrac{-2}{5}$, y-intercept = $\dfrac{7}{5}$

3.   Find the slope of the line in the graph below

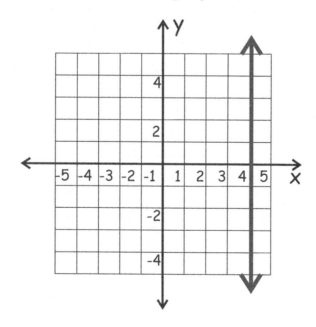

(A) -1   (B) Undefined   (C) 1   (D) 2

4.   Which of the below order pair is the solution for the below system of equations ?

$$8p - 9q = 27$$
$$p + 9q = 54$$

(A) (9 , 5)   (B) (5 , -9)   (C) (0 , 5)   (D) (-9, -3)

5.   Solve the Following Inequality ?
                    -3 (6 - 3m) <= -81

(A) m <= -15   (B) m >= 25   (C) m <= -7   (D) m >= -5

6.   The equation of the line 'm' is represented by which of the below options ?

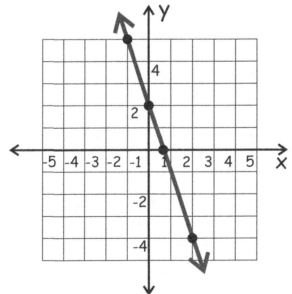

(A) y = -2x + 2   (B) y = 3x - 2

(C) y = 4x + 2   (D) y = -2x - 2

50   www.a4ace.com   www.math-knots.com

7.　Which of the below quadratic equation has roots of 6 and 7 ?

$\quad$ (A) $y^2 + 13y = -42$
$\quad$ (B) $y^2 - y = -42$
$\quad$ (C) $y^2 + y = -42$
$\quad$ (D) $y^2 - 13y = -42$

8.　Which Graph best represents the equation

$$Y = -2$$

(A)

(B)

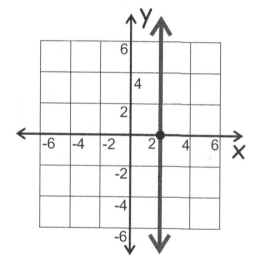

(C)

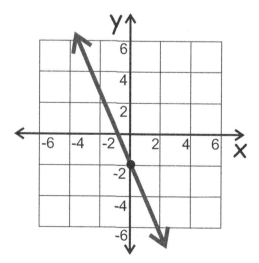

(D)

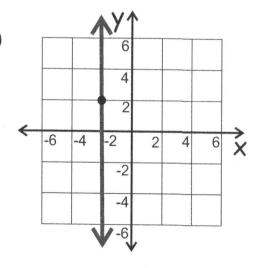

　　　　　　www.a4ace.com　　　www.math-knots.com

9. System of linear equations are shown in the graph below. Which of the below is the solution of the system of linear equations ?

    $y = 4x + 1$

    $y = -3x + 8$

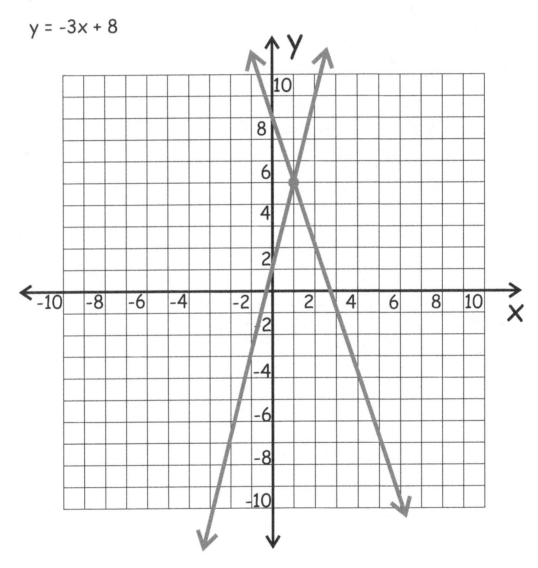

(A) (10 , 1)   (B) (1 , -5)

(C) (1 , 5)   (D) (1 , 10)

52   www.a4ace.com   www.math-knots.com

10. Which of the below represents distributive property

    (A) $4(8 - 6z) = (8 + 6z)4$ (B) $4(8 + 6z) = 2(8 + 6z)$

    (C) $-4(5z + 7) = 20m + 12$ (D) $4(8 + 6z) = 32 + 24z$

11. Which of the below graphs represents the equation of the straight line
    represented as

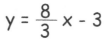

$$y = \frac{8}{3}x - 3$$

(A)

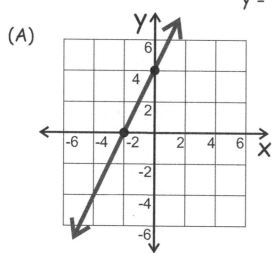

(B)

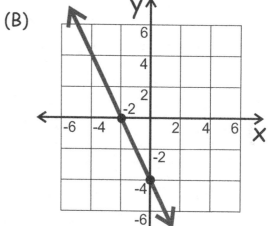

(C)

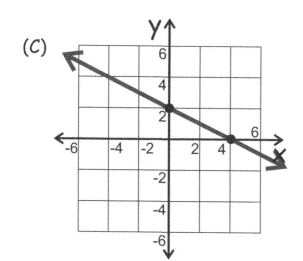

(D)

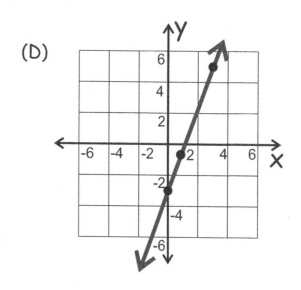

12. Imagination team raises funds for the local hospital. They sell baked cookies for $2 each and the ingredients to make the cookies costed $171. If p is the profit and K is the number of cookies sold as shown by the given equation

$$P = 2K - 171$$

What is the slope of the equation ?

(A) 2   (B) -171

(C) 171   (D) -2

13. Roots of the below equation are

$$n^2 + 7n + 6 = 0$$

(A)   (-5 , -1)
(B)   (-4 , 1)
(C)   (-6 , -1)
(D)   (-6 , 2)

14. Find the equation of the straight line with slope $= \dfrac{-1}{2}$ and containing the point (-6 , 1)

(A) $y = \dfrac{-x}{2} + 2$ (B) $y = \dfrac{x}{2} + 6$

(C) $y = \dfrac{x}{2} - 7$ (D) $y = \dfrac{-x}{2} - 2$

     54   www.a4ace.com   www.math-knots.com

15. Which of the below inequalities is same as 6m - 3n <= 21

(A)   n <= 5 - 8m/3

(B)   n >= 2m -7

(C)   n <= 2m -3

(D)   n <= 2m - 7

16. What is the slope of the line that passes through

(-6 , -12) , (8 , -12)

(A) $\dfrac{3}{5}$

(B) $-\dfrac{3}{5}$

(C)   Undefined

(D)   0

17. James spent half of his weekly allowance this weekend to watch a movie with friends. He mowed lawn and earned $15. What was his weekly allowance if he has $ 43 now ?

(A) 56

(B) 36

(C) 41

(D) 3

18. Tony's garage charges Sam an amount of $26 for 5 tire changes and 2 wiper changes. They charge Ken $11 for 2 tire changes and a wiper change What is the cost of one wiper change ?

   (A) $4 (B) $2.90

   (C) $3 (D) $3.40

19. Evaluate $\dfrac{q + mp^3}{4}$; Where m = -4, p = -4, and q = -8

   (A) 62 (B) 66

   (C) 72 (D) 68

20. Evaluate

$$(6.43 \times 10^8) \ (2.9 \times 10^0)$$

   (A) 2.217×10^7 (B) 0.1865×10^{10}

   (C) 1.865×10^{11} (D) 1.865×10^{-11}

21. Simplify the expression

$$(4b - 7b^4 - 6b^3) + (2b - 4 - 2b^4) - (4b^4 - 8 + 8b^3)$$

(A) $-13b^4 - 14b^3 + 6b + 4$

(B) $13b^4 + 14b^3 - 13b^2 - 4$

(C) $19b^4 - 4b^3 - 13b^2 - 4$

(D) $11b^4 - 14b^3 - 6b + 4$

22. Simplest radical form of $\sqrt{1083}$ is ?

(A) $17\sqrt{3}$

(B) 17

(C) 19

(D) $19\sqrt{3}$

23. Evaluate the polynomial to simplest form where $x \neq 0$

$$(4a^4 + 2a^3 + 8a^2) \div 4a$$

(A) $4 + \dfrac{2}{3a} + \dfrac{2}{2a^2}$

(B) $a^3 + \dfrac{a^2}{2} + 2a$

(C) $4a^4 + \dfrac{a^3}{4} + 4a^2$

(D) $\dfrac{a^3}{4} + a^2 + a$

24. Factorize the below quadratic expression completely ?

$$5p^2 + 18p - 35$$

(A) $(5p - 7)(p - 5)$

(B) $(5p + 7)(p - 5)$

(C) $(2p + 3)(p + 10)$

(D) $(5p - 7)(p + 5)$

25. The product of m and 11 is 25

(A) $11m = 25$

(B) $m^{11} = 25$

(C) $11 - m = 25$

(D) $m - 11 = 25$

26. Evaluate the polynomial

$$6k (5k^2 + 6k + 2)$$

(A) $35k^2 + 40k - 5$

(B) $30k^3 + 36k^2 + 12k$

(C) $14k^3 + 4k^2 + 16k$

(D) $20k^4 + 20k^3 + 25k^2$

27. Which labeled point on the number line is closest to sqrt (104) ?

(A)   U   (B)   T   (C)   P   (D) R

28. A flag pole is of length 75567×10^{-3} when standing on the ground. It is installed at the depth of 9321×10^{-3}. How high is the flag from the ground ?

(A) 662.46×10^{-1}

(B) 0.662×10^{-6}

(C) 66.246×10^{0}

(D) 66.2×10^{-6}

29. Factorize the below quadratic expression completely ?

$$-63r^2 + 7r$$

(A) $35(-9r + 4)$

(B) $r^2 (-9r + 1)$

(C) $7r^2 (-9r^2 + 1)$

(D) $7r (-9r + 1)$

30. The cube of a number is equal to 44

(A) $3^3 = 44$

(B) $n + 3 \geq 44$

(C) $n^3 = 44$

(D) $\dfrac{3n^3}{2} = 44$

31. The function f(X) = $50 - X ; Daisy buys a video game for $19. She gives the cashier $50. With how much money does she get back ?

(A) $30

(B) $31

(C) $50

(D) $19

32. Which of the below equation represents the relationship between time and Cookies made with an additional preparation time of 45 minutes ?

Time in minutes (t)	# cookies (c)
3	12
4	16
8	32
10	40
24	96

(A) c = 4t + 45

(B) c = 45 - 4t

(C) c = 4t/45

(D) c = 4t - 45

33. Find the domain of the relation shown from the below data set ?

X	Y
0.1	0.01
0.5	0.9
0.6	56.2
0.7	75.1
0.22	96.2

(A) { 0.1 , 0.5 , 0.6 , 0.7 , 0.22 }

(B) { -0.3 , -0.1 , 1.3 , 0.9 , 0.22 }

(C) { 0.1 , 0.7 , 0.22 , 75.1 , 96.2 }

(D) { 0.01 , 0.9 , 56.2 , 75.1 , 96.2 }

34. If 32 yards of cloth is required to stitch 16 skirts, how much cloth is required to stitch 50 skirts ?

   (A) 110 yards   (B) 100 yards

   (C) 450 yards   (D) 466 yards

35. Which of the below order pairs data set represents a function ?

   (A) { (74 , 31) , (65 , 35.4) , (73 , 40.4) , (74 , 39.8) , (84 , 44.4) }

   (B) { (57 , 31) , (65 , 35.4) , (84 , 40.4) , (74 , 39.8) , (84 , 44.4) }

   (C) { (57 , 31) , (65 , 35.4) , (73 , 40.4) , (74 , 39.8) , (65 , 44.4) }

   (D) { (57 , 31) , (65 , 35.4) , (73 , 40.4) , (74 , 39.8) , (84 , 44.4) }

36. Evaluate f(7), where $f(x) = x^2 + 4x - 15$

   (A) 62

   (B) 54

   (C) 37

   (D) 64

37. What is the domain of the function y = x - 2 represented by the
below graph ?

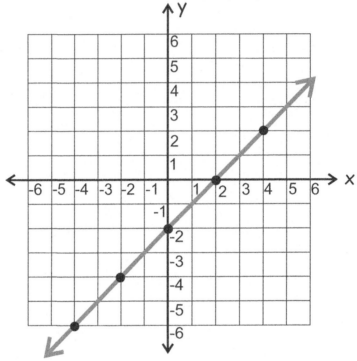

(A)   D = {0 , -1 , -2 , - 5 , -3 }

(B)   D = {3 , 4.1 , 13.7 , -21 , 3.9 }

(C)   D = {0 , 2 , 4 , -2 , -4 }

(D)   D = {0 , 0.5 , -8 , - 7 , -11 }

38. What is the range of the function f(x) = x^3 - 7
where Domain = { -5 , -2 , 1 , 3}

(A) { 132 , 15 , -6 , -20 }   (B) { -132 , -1 , 6 , 20 }

(C) { 108 , -1 , -6 , 20 }   (D) { -15 , -6 , 20 , -132 }

39. Which graph best represents a direct variation ?

$$y = -2x$$

(A)
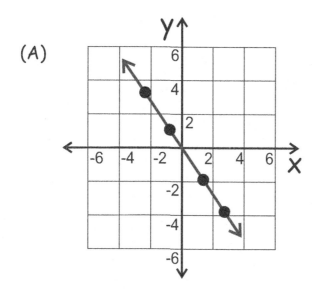

(B)
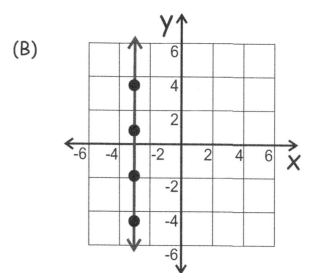

(C)
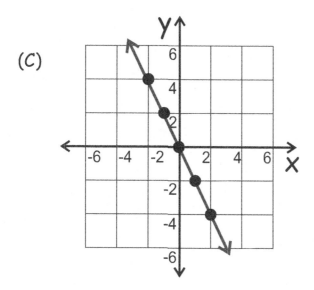

(D)
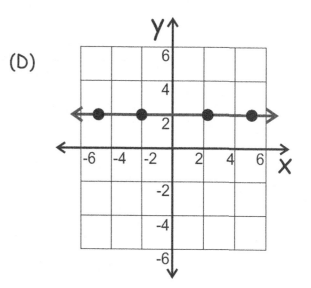

40. Which of the below tables shows the relation between X and Y as direct variation ?

(A)

X	Y
1	37
2	21
3	73
4	91
5	15

(B)

X	Y
1	19
2	24
3	35
4	61
5	67

(C)

X	Y
1	17
2	24
3	37
4	29
5	41

(D)

X	Y
1	7
2	14
3	21
4	28
5	35

41. Cost of each STEM kit in the STEAM expo is shown in the below table with a flat rate of $3.25 sales tax on each order.

# of STEMkit(S)	Sale Price $(P)
1	19
3	57
8	152
10	190
12	228

Which of the below gives the total price (t) if we order S STEM kits in one order ?

(A) t = 3.25s - 19

(B) t = 3.25s + 19

(C) t = 22.25s

(D) t = 19s + 3.25

42. Which of the below graph best represents the function $f(x) = x^2 - 5x + 4$

(A)

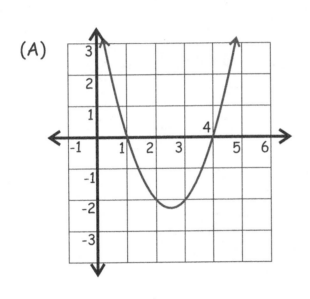

(B)

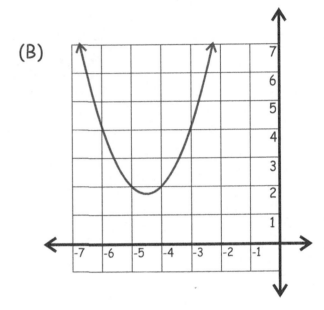

(C)

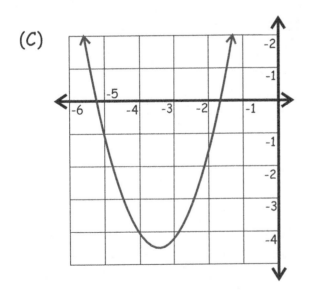

(D)

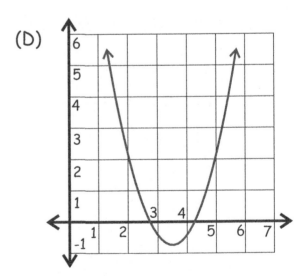

43. Find the sum of the below Matrices ?

$$
\begin{vmatrix} 5 & 8 \\ 11 & -4 \\ 7 & 9 \end{vmatrix} + \begin{vmatrix} 7 & 1 \\ -3 & -7 \\ 1 & 15 \end{vmatrix}
$$

(A) $\begin{vmatrix} 11 & 8 \\ 5 & -10 \\ 1 & -5 \end{vmatrix}$ (B) $\begin{vmatrix} 12 & 9 \\ 8 & -11 \\ 8 & 24 \end{vmatrix}$

(C) $\begin{vmatrix} 5 & 7 \\ -7 & 8 \\ 10 & 6 \end{vmatrix}$ (D) $\begin{vmatrix} 15 & 10 \\ -10 & 6 \\ 26 & -8 \end{vmatrix}$

44. The table below shows the XYZ car sales in various stores in Virginia

December car sales

Day	Store#1	Store#2	Store#3	Store#4
Monday	21	17	11	38
Tuesday	12	38	34	16
Wednesday	17	19	10	2
Thursday	20	5	91	15
Friday	43	19	44	37
Saturday	25	55	15	23
Sunday	40	43	20	58

Which store sold the highest average number of cars this week ?

(A) Store #2

(B) Store # 3

(C) Store # 1

(D) Store # 4

45. Which equation is the line of best fit for the data in the below table ?

x	y
0	-5
2	-4.5
8	-3
20	0
24	1

(A) Y = $\frac{x}{4}$ - 2

(B) Y = $\frac{x}{2}$ - 5

(C) Y = $\frac{x}{4}$ - 5

(D) Y = $\frac{x}{4}$ + 5

46. Which graph best represents the below data ?

STEM Teams

Team Name	Games won
Black Panthers	4
Charges	10
Chaos	10
Defenders	1
Enforcers	1
Gunners	1
Soldiers	22
Soul takers	31
Navy	11
The blazers	15
The frontline	8
The tribe	1
Veterans	2

Team Name	Games won
Occupiers	17
Achievers	8
Performers	17
Professionals	28
Pythons	3
The generals	7
The leaders	30
Urban Kings	4
Unbeatables	29

(A)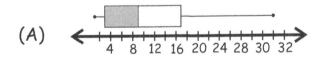

(B)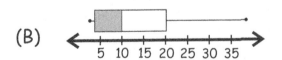

(C)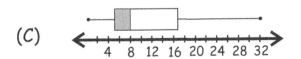

(D)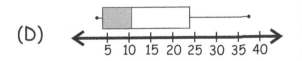

47. Which is most likely the best fit for the below equation ?

$$y = x + 6$$

(A)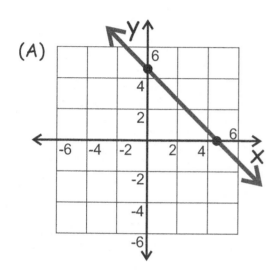

(B)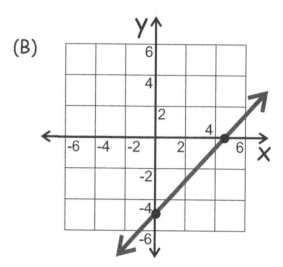

(C)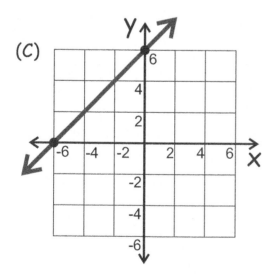

(D)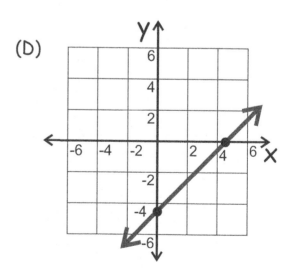

48. Jane solved below number of puzzles each week

30 , 88 , 83 , 93 , 61

He then solved 71 more after the week . How are the mean and median affected ?

(A) The mean and the median both decreased.
(B) The median decreased and the mean is increased.
(C) The median and the mean both remained the same.
(D) The mean remains same and median decreased.

49. Comfy wear shoe store has a sale and charges a flat rate of $82
The table below shows various ages and the number of shoes sold.

Shoe size	# pairs sold	Shoe size	# pairs sold
7 - 10	17	19 - 22	434
11 - 14	66	23 - 26	97
15 - 18	101	27 - 30	192

Which of the below represents the total money collected ?

(A)
$$20 \begin{vmatrix} 15 & 192 \\ 97 & 64 \\ 101 & 70 \end{vmatrix}$$

(B)
$$28 \begin{vmatrix} 21 & 57 \\ 192 & 66 \\ 101 & 97 \end{vmatrix}$$

(C)
$$82 \begin{vmatrix} 17 & 434 \\ 66 & 97 \\ 101 & 192 \end{vmatrix}$$

(B)
$$82 \begin{vmatrix} 66 & 97 \\ 192 & 101 \\ 77 & 434 \end{vmatrix}$$

**ALGEBRA 1
MATH SOL**

50. Evaluate the below matrices

$$
\begin{vmatrix} 6 & 5 \\ 4 & 3 \\ 2 & 1 \end{vmatrix} + \begin{vmatrix} 12 & 11 \\ 10 & 9 \\ 12 & 13 \end{vmatrix} = ?
$$

(A) $\begin{vmatrix} 14 & 7 \\ 2 & -13 \\ 15 & -21 \end{vmatrix}$

(B) $\begin{vmatrix} -9 & 15 \\ 7 & 17 \\ 15 & -1 \end{vmatrix}$

(C) $\begin{vmatrix} -15 & -2 \\ 6 & 3 \\ -3 & 4 \end{vmatrix}$

(D) $\begin{vmatrix} 18 & 16 \\ 14 & 12 \\ 14 & 14 \end{vmatrix}$

         www.a4ace.com   www.math-knots.com

ALGEBRA 1
SOL
Practice Test - 6

1.   Solve for v

$$3v + (-4 (1 - 2v)) = 3 (3v + 4)$$

(A) -11   (B) 8   (C) 7   (D) 0

2.   If f(k) = 99k + 101 then which of the below best describes the graph f(k)

(A) Slope = 99 , y-intercept = 101
(B) Slope = - 101 , y-intercept = 99
(C) Slope = - 99 , y-intercept = 101
(D) Slope = 101 , y-intercept = -99

3.   Find the slope of the line in the graph below

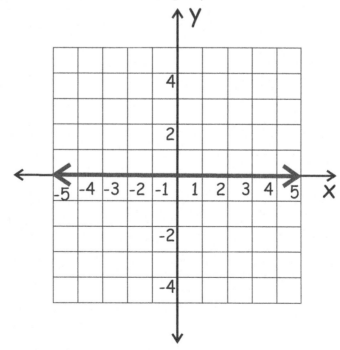

(A) $\frac{-1}{3}$ (B) $\frac{-5}{3}$ (C) $\frac{1}{3}$ (D) 0

                   www.a4ace.com   www.math-knots.com

4.   Which of the below order pair is the solution of the below system of
     equations ?

$$10p - 3q = -18$$
$$2p - 3q = 6$$

   (A) (-3, 2)   (B) (-3, -2)   (C) (-3, -4)   (D) (3, 4)

5. $4p + (-7 (3p + 2)) <= 88$

   (A) p >= -6   (B) p >= -27

   (C) p <= -22   (D) p >= -40

6.   The equation of the line 'm' is represented by which of the below options ?

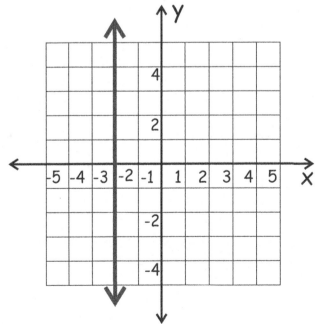

   (A) x = -2   (B) x = 3x - 2   (C) x = 4x + 2   (D) x = -2x + 3

7. Which of the below quadratic equation has roots of 0 and 5 ?

(A m^2 - 5m - 35 = 35   (B) m^2 - 5m - 35 = +35

(C) m^2 - 5m - 35 = -35   (D) m^2 + 5m - 35 = -35

8. Which Graph best represents the equation ?

$$Y = -x + 6$$

(A)
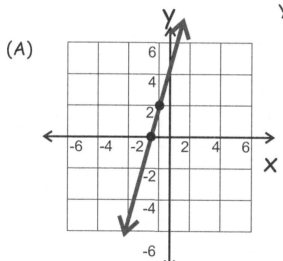

(B)
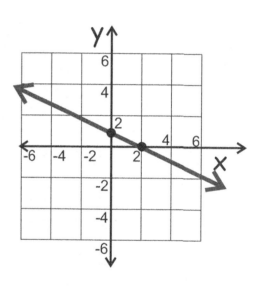

(C)
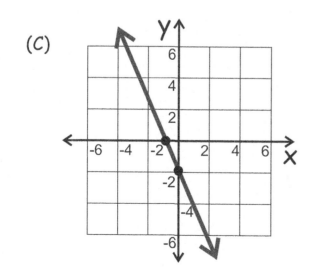

(D)
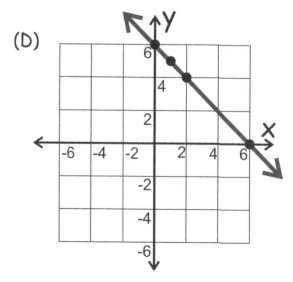

9. System of linear equations are shown in the graph below. Which of the below is the solution of the system of linear equations ?

$$y = -\frac{3}{2}x - 2$$

$$y = -\frac{1}{4}x - 7$$

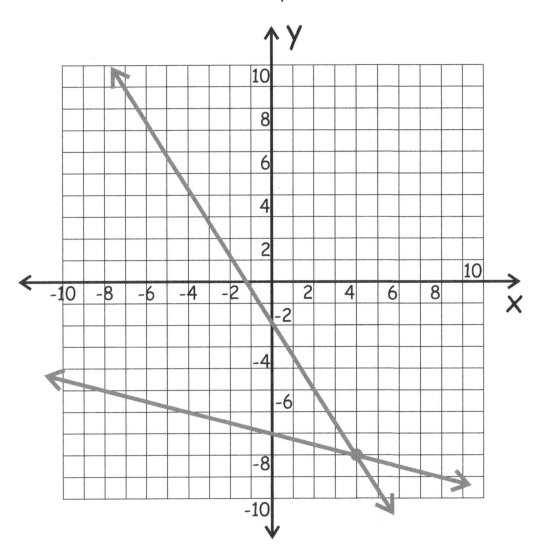

(A) (-1 , 4)

(B) (-8 , 4)

(C) (4 , -8)

(D) (-4 , -1)

10. Which of the below represents distributive property ?

   (A) $7(2m + 5) = (2m + 5)7$ (B) $7(2m + 5) = 14m + 35$

   (C) $7(2m + 5) = 7(2m - 5)$ (D) $(2m + 5) = 5 + 2m$

11. Which of the below graphs represents the equation of the straight line represented as $y = -\dfrac{9}{4}x + 6$

(A)
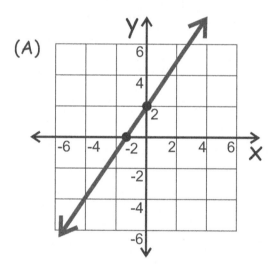

(B)
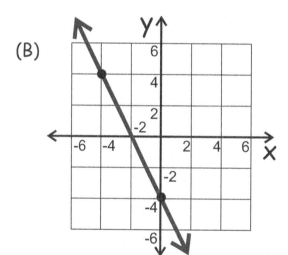

(C)
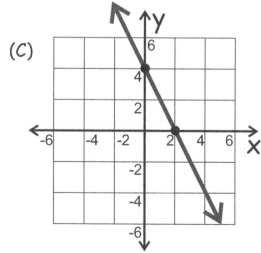

(D)
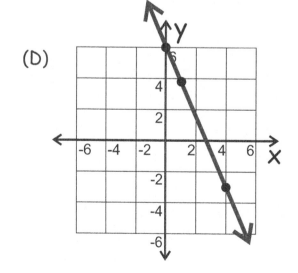

12. Jason buys a laptop for $2105 by taking loan from the store and pays only interest every month. He also lends $355 every month from his mother. After m months the amount he owes in debts is given by the equation

$$d = -355m - 2105$$

What is the slope of the equation?

(A) 355

(B) –355

(C) 2105

(D) –2105

13. Roots of the below equation are

$$3p^2 - 6 = -3p$$

(A) (-5 , -1)
(B) (-6 , -1)
(C) (1 , -2)
(D) (-6 , 2)

14. Find the equation of the straight line with slope = 5 and containing the point (-4 , -20)

(A) s = 5p

(B) s = 5p - 2

(C) s = $\dfrac{5p}{2}$

(D) s = 5p + 2

 www.a4ace.com   www.math-knots.com

15. Which of the below inequalities is same as 5 (-7n + 2p) <= -105

(A) $n >= 3 + \dfrac{2p}{7}$

(B) $n >= 3 - \dfrac{2p}{7}$

(C) $n >= \dfrac{2p}{7} - 3$

(D) n <= 3 - 2m

16. What is the slope of the line that passes through (-19 , 13) , (-10 , -14) ?

(A) 3

(B) $-\dfrac{1}{3}$

(C) -3

(D) $\dfrac{1}{3}$

17. 300 reduced by 3 times my number is 84. What is my number ?

(A) 75

(B) 66

(C) 72

(D) 54

18. A store sells two shirts and 3 pants for $26. The same store sells two shirts and a pant for $17. What is the price of the shirt at the store ?

(A) $7.70

(B) $6.50

(C) $3.50

(D) $6.25

19.   Evaluate

$p - (r - (p - (q - 4)))$; Where $p = -6$, $q = 8$ and $r = -2$

(A) -18   (B) -11

(C) -14   (D) -16

20.   Evaluate $\dfrac{5.93 \times 10^5}{9.2 \times 10^2}$

(A) 6.446×10^2 (B) 6.446×10^{-2}

(C) 5.456×10^8 (D) 5.456×10^9

21.   Simplify the expression

$(3r^4 - 7r^2 - 5r^3) + (8r^4 - 8r^2 - 4r^3) + (5r^3 - 4 + 2r^2)$

(A) $13r^4 - 4r^3 - 13r^2 - 4$ (B) $19r^4 + r^3 - 13r^2 - 4$

(C) $19r^4 - 4r^3 - 13r^2 - 4$ (D) $11r^4 - 4r^3 - 13r^2 - 4$

22.   Simplest radical form of $\sqrt{1681}$ is ?

(A) 49   (B) 41

(C) 39   (D) 27

23. Evaluate the polynomial to simplest form where $x \neq 0$

$$(2a^3 + 4a^2 + a) \div 4$$

(A) $\dfrac{a^3}{2} + 3a + \dfrac{1}{8}$

(B) $\dfrac{a^3}{4} + \dfrac{a^2}{4} + a$

(C) $2 + \dfrac{2}{a} + \dfrac{3}{8a^2}$

(D) $\dfrac{a^3}{2} + a^2 + \dfrac{a}{4}$

24. Factorize the below quadratic expression completely ?

$$10c^2 + 52c + 10$$

(A) None

(B) $2(5c + 1)(c + 5)$

(C) $2(5c - 1)(c - 5)$

(D) $5(c + 1)^2$

25. p to the 4th power is less than 16

(A) $4p < 16$

(B) $4^p < 16$

(C) $p^4 < 16$

(D) $\dfrac{4}{p} < 16$

     www.a4ace.com   www.math-knots.com

26. Evaluate the polynomial

$$4a^2 (2a^2 + 8a + 7)$$

(A) $2a^3 - 4a^2 - 12a$ (B) $8a^4 + 32a^3 + 28a^2$

(C) $56a^2 + 8a + 16$ (D) $2a^2 + 120 + 16$

27. Which labeled point on the number line is closest to $\sqrt{488}$

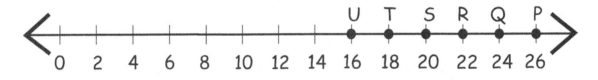

(A) U   (B) P

(C) S   (D) R

28. Height of two buildings in Chicago down town of lengths 77221.34×10^{-3} and 71219.07×10^{-3}. What is the difference between the two buildings ?

(A) 6.02×10^{-4} (B) 6002×10^{-3}

(C) 0.6002×10^{-3} (D) 600.1×10^{-3}

29. Factorize the below quadratic expression completely ?

$$6b^2 - 2b$$

(A) $2b(3b^2 - b)$

(B) $2b (3b - 1)$

(C) $2b^2 (3b^2 - 1)$

(D) $2 (3b^3 - b)$

30. Seven less than p is equal to thirty three

(A) $\frac{7}{2} = 33$

(B) $7 - p \geq 33$

(C) $7 - p = 33$

(D) $p - 7 = 33$

31. The function f(X) = 30X + 25 ; X = Number of hours he worked. Matt has a saving of $25. If he works for ten hours this week, how much money does he have now ?

(A) $325

(B) $365

(C) $350

(D) $455

87   www.a4ace.com   www.math-knots.com

32. Which of the below equation represents the relationship between time and book stacking in the library ?

Time in minutes (t)	# books stacked (b)
3	27
4	36
8	72
10	90
24	216

(A) $b = 9 + t$ (B) $b = \dfrac{t}{9}$ (C) $b = 9t$ (D) $b = \dfrac{6}{t}$

33. Find the domain of the relation shown from the below data set ?

x	y
0.9	0.1
0.7	0.6
0.3	23.8
0.1	134
0.2	34.1

(A) { 0.9 , -0.7 , 23.8 , 0.1 , -0.2}

(B) { 0.9 , -0.7 , 0.3 , 134 , 0.2}

(C) { -0.9 , 0.7 , 0.3 , -0.1 , 34.1}

(D) { 0.9 , 0.7 , 0.3 , 0.1 , 0.2}

34. An electric bulb consumes 3 units of electricity if it is switched on continuously for 18 hours. How much electricity does it consume if it is switched on for 42 hours ?

(A) 7
(B) 4
(C) 10
(D) 15

35. Which of the below order pairs data set represents a function ?

(A) { (4 , 6) , (5.7 , 6) , (7.8 , 18) , (12.1 , 23) , (17.3 , 45) }

(B) { (4 , 6) , (5.7 , 6) , (7.8 , 18) , (7.8 , 23) , (17.3 , 45) }

(C) { (4 , 6) , (5.7 , 6) , (7.8 , 18) , (5.7 , 23) , (17.3 , 45) }

(D) { (4 , 6) , (5.7 , 6) , (7.8 , 18) , (12.1 , 23) , (4 , 45) }

36. Evaluate f(11), where $f(x) = x^2 + 2x - 25$

(A) 129

(B) 137

(C) 118

(D) 231

37. What is the domain of the function y = x - 3 represented by the below graph ?

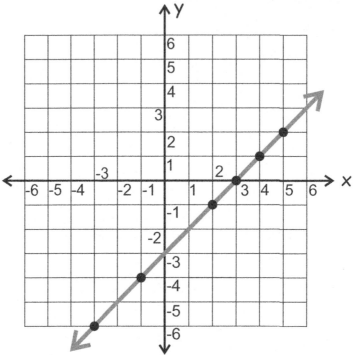

(A) D = {0, 1 , 2 , - 5 , -3 }

(B) D = {-6 , -5 , -4 , 2.2 , 5 }

(C) D = {-3 , -1 , 2 , 3 , 4 , 5 }

(D) D = {-9 , 2.5 , 4.5 , - 8 , -15 }

38. What is the range of the function $f(x) = 2x^5 - 11$
     where Domain = { -2 , -1 , 0 , 2}

(A) { 75 , 13 , -11 , 33}   (B) { -75 , -13 , -11 , 53}

(C) { 75 , -103 , -111 , -33}   (D) { 75 , 13 , 11 , 33}

                   www.a4ace.com   www.math-knots.com

39. Which graph best represents   y = -3x + 1

(A)

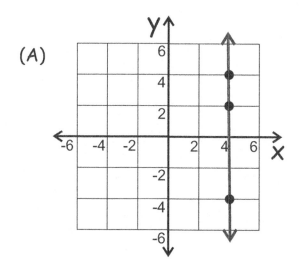

(B)

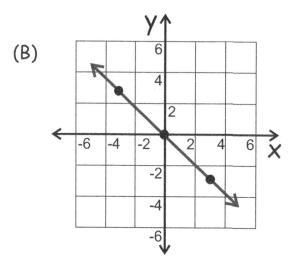

(C)

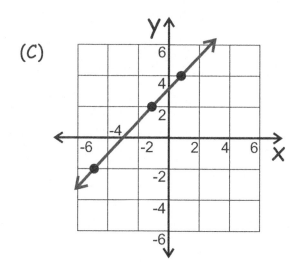

(D)

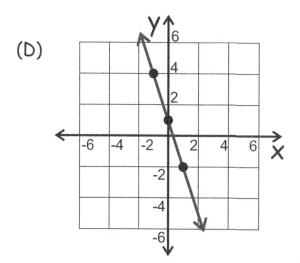

www.a4ace.com   www.math-knots.com

40. Which of the below tables shows the relation between X and Y as direct variation.

(A)

x	y
2	6
4	12
6	18
10	30
12	36

(B)

x	y
2	8
4	11
6	18
10	27
12	31

(C)

x	y
2	16
4	12
6	38
10	41
12	50

(D)

x	y
2	25
4	12
6	62
10	30
12	37
2	6

41. Yummy Yummy Cup cake store sells each one at a flat rate of $1.85 with an extra charge for toppings chosen as below

# Cup cake toppings (p)	Sale Price $(s)
0	1.85
1	2.10
3	2.60
8	3.85
10	4.35

Which of the below gives the total price (t) of p toppings ?

(A) t = 3.75p - 0.5s

(B) t = 3.4p - 0.5

(C) t = 4.25p

(D) t = 1.85 + 0.25p

42.   Which of the below graph best represents the function $f(x) = -x^2$

(A)
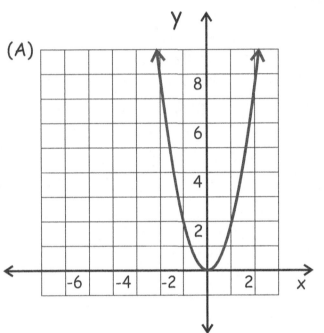

(B)
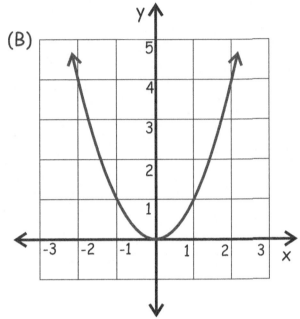

(C)
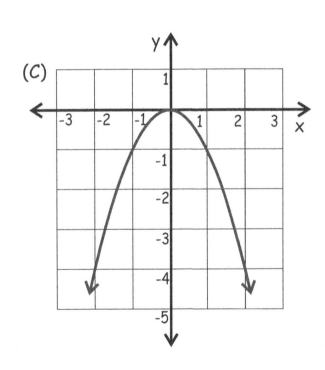

(D)
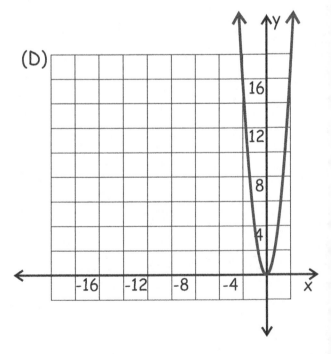

43. Find the sum of the below Matrices ?

$$
\begin{vmatrix} 10 & 7 \\ 16 & 2 \\ 0 & -12 \end{vmatrix} + \begin{vmatrix} -6 & 4 \\ 9 & 5 \\ 1 & 6 \end{vmatrix}
$$

(A)
$$
\begin{vmatrix} 4 & 11 \\ 25 & 7 \\ 1 & -6 \end{vmatrix}
$$

(B)
$$
\begin{vmatrix} 8 & 18 \\ -4 & 15 \\ 11 & 7 \end{vmatrix}
$$

(C)
$$
\begin{vmatrix} 5 & 7 \\ -17 & 8 \\ 10 & 27 \end{vmatrix}
$$

(D)
$$
\begin{vmatrix} 1 & 15 \\ -6 & 17 \\ 25 & -8 \end{vmatrix}
$$

44. The table below shows the number of scarfs made by each class of Art elementary school for a fundraiser sales that is upcoming.

Scarfs made by 8th grade

Day	Class#1	Class#2	Class#3	Class#4
Monday	91	11	21	31
Tuesday	37	21	43	99
Wednesday	15	47	27	38
Thursday	29	45	55	42
Friday	31	32	88	75

Which sixth grade class made the highest number of scarfs for the fund raiser ?

(A) Class #2

(B) Class # 3

(C) Class # 1

(D) Class # 4

45. Which equation is the line of best fit for the data in the below table ?

x	y
-1	16
2	1
4	-9
-2	21
3	-4

(A) Y = -5X + 11

(B) Y = -5X - 11

(C) Y = -5X + 5

(D) Y = 5X + 11

www.a4ace.com   www.math-knots.com

46. Which graph best represents the below data ?

Average lifespan

Animal	Years
Leopard	17
Canvasback duck	19
Rainbow lorikeet	15
Cobra	28
Amazon parrot	47
American toad	15
Nutria	15
Tiger	11
Bee	15
Bull frogs	12
Bull	16
Flying squirell	28
Salamander	14
Teal	4

Animal	Years
Eagle	47
Bison	30
Tasmanian Tiger	7
Crocodile	45
Chicken	15
sian elephant	40
Rabit	9
Dogs	15

(A)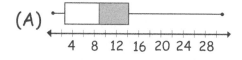

(B)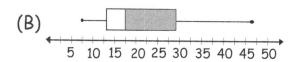

(C)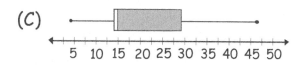

(D)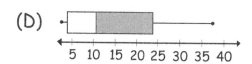

47. Which is most likely the best fit for the below equation ?

$$y = 2x + 3$$

(A)

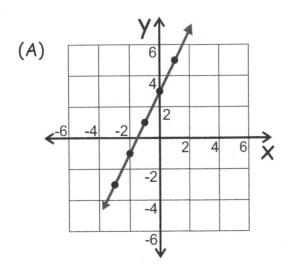

(B)

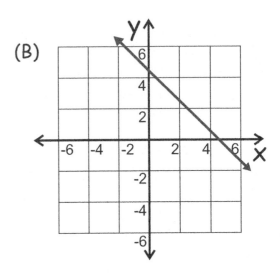

(C)

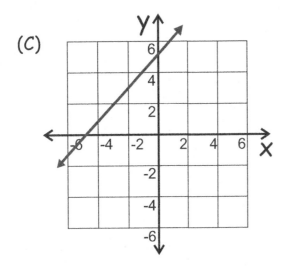

(D)

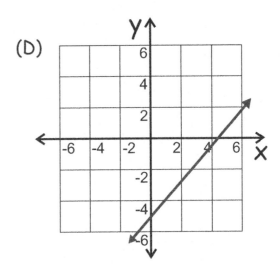

www.a4ace.com   www.math-knots.com

48. A yummy fruit store charges a flat rate of $3. The table below shows various fruits and the number of pounds that were sold this week

Fruit type	Pounds	Fruit type	Pounds
Straw berries	21	Apples	57
Blue berries	05	Pears	13
Grapes	61	Oranges	49

Which of the below represents the total money collected ?

(A)
$$8 \begin{vmatrix} 25 & 55 \\ 11 & 47 \\ 38 & 35 \end{vmatrix}$$

(B)
$$3 \begin{vmatrix} 21 & 57 \\ 5 & 13 \\ 61 & 49 \end{vmatrix}$$

(C)
$$13 \begin{vmatrix} 5 & 12 \\ 7 & 15 \\ 9 & 15 \end{vmatrix}$$

(D)
$$5 \begin{vmatrix} 55 & 32 \\ 48 & 41 \\ 63 & 59 \end{vmatrix}$$

49. Tim's car sales each week over last 4 weeks in summer are shown
    73, 55, 91, 69
    He then sold 72 more cars. How are the mean and median affected ?

    (A) The mean increased and the median remained the same.
    (B) The median increased and the mean remained the same.
    (C) The median and the mean both remained the same.
    (D) The mean and the median both decreased.

     www.a4ace.com   www.math-knots.com

50. Evaluate the below matrices

$$
\begin{vmatrix} -1 & 5 \\ -3 & -6 \\ 2 & -4 \end{vmatrix} + \begin{vmatrix} 10 & -8 \\ -7 & 11 \\ -9 & 17 \end{vmatrix} = \ ?
$$

(A) $\begin{vmatrix} -9 & 15 \\ 7 & 17 \\ 15 & -1 \end{vmatrix}$

(B) $\begin{vmatrix} -15 & -2 \\ 6 & 3 \\ -3 & 4 \end{vmatrix}$

(C) $\begin{vmatrix} 14 & 7 \\ 2 & -13 \\ 15 & -21 \end{vmatrix}$

(D) $\begin{vmatrix} 9 & -3 \\ -10 & 5 \\ -7 & 13 \end{vmatrix}$

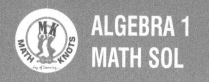

ALGEBRA 1
SOL
Practice Test - 4
Answer Keys

 www.a4ace.com   www.math-knots.com

Answer Key Test - 4

1. D

2. B

3. D

4. C

5. B

6. A

7. A

8. D

9. B

10. C

11. C

12. C

13. B

14. D

15. A

103

16. C

17. B

18. A

19. D

20. C

21. D

22. A

23. D

24. C

25. D

26. C

27. D

28. A

29. D

30. B

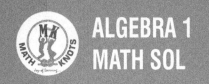
31. A

32. A

33. C

34. B

35. D

36. C

37. A

38. C

39. D

40. C

41. A

42. A

43. D

44. C

45. A

46. C

47.   A

48.   B

49.   A

50.   C

ALGEBRA 1
SOL
Practice Test - 5
Answer Keys

<u>Answer Key Test - 5</u>

1.   D

2.   C

3.   B

4.   A

5.   C

6.   A

7.   D

8.   A

9.   C

10.   D

11.   D

12.   A

13.   C

14.   D

15.   B

     www.a4ace.com   www.math-knots.com

16. D

17. A

18. C

19. B

20. B

21. A

22. D

23. B

24. D

25. A

26. B

27. D

28. A

29. D

30. C

31. B

32. A

33. A

34. B

35. D

36. A

37. C

38. D

39. C

40. D

41. D

42. A

43. B

44. B

45. C

46. A

47. C

48. D

49. C

50. D

ALGEBRA 1
SOL
Practice Test - 6
Answer Keys

www.a4ace.com   www.math-knots.com

www.a4ace.com   www.math-knots.com

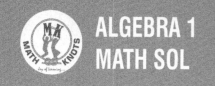
Answer Key Test - 6

1. B

2. A

3. D

4. C

5. A

6. A

7. C

8. D

9. C

10. B

11. D

12. B

13. C

14. A

15. A

16. C

17. C

18. D

19. C

20. A

21. D

22. B

23. D

24. B

25. C

26. B

27. D

28. B

29. B

30. D

31. A

32. C

33. D

34. A

35. A

36. C

37. C

38. B

39. D

40. A

41. D

42. C

43. A

44. D

45. A

46. C

     www.a4ace.com   www.math-knots.com

47.   A

48.   B

49.   B

50.   D

ALGEBRA 1
SOL
Score Calculation

Algebra 1 Score calculation

If you get this many times correct :	Then your converted scale scor is :
0	000
1	217
2	249
3	268
4	282
5	293
6	303
7	311
8	319
9	325
10	331
11	337
12	343
13	348
14	353
15	357
16	362
17	366
18	371
19	375

20	379
21	383
22	387
23	391
24	395
25	399
26	403
27	407
28	411
29	415
30	419
31	423
32	427
33	432
34	436
35	441
36	445
37	450
38	456
39	461

40	467
41	473
42	480
43	487
44	496
45	505
46	516
47	531
48	550
49	582
50	600

Made in the USA
Middletown, DE
24 April 2022